PRO-ROLLER®

MASSAGE ESSENTIALS

THIRD EDITION

Angela Kneale
OTD, MA, OTR/L, NBC-HWC

Occupational Therapist
Integrative Health and Wellness Coach
Certified Pilates Instructor
Franklin Method® Educator

PRO-ROLLER® Massage Essentials, **Third Edition**

Published by:
OPTP
Tools for fitness. Knowledge for health.
3800 Annapolis Lane, Suite 165
Minneapolis, Minnesota 55447
800.367.7393
OPTP.com

Printed in the United States of America

Cover and Interior Design: OPTP
Editor: Marly Cornell
Technical Editor: Susanne Schaars, MSPT, Dip.MDT
Photography: TJ Thoraldson Photography
Photo Production: Dani Hartmann
Digital Imaging: Anna Rajdl
PRO-ROLLER Model: Karlee Ann Callender

ISBN: 978-1-942798-15-6

Every effort has been made to ensure that the information contained in this publication is accurate and current at the time of printing. The ideas, exercises, and suggestions are not intended as a substitute for consulting with your healthcare provider. All matters regarding your health require medical supervision. Neither the author nor the publisher shall be liable or responsible for any loss, injury, or damage allegedly arising from any information or suggestion in this publication.

Information in this publication is intended only for general health knowledge. Nothing in this publication should be considered personal medical advice.

Before taking any actions that will affect your health, consult your physician or knowledgeable healthcare professional to discuss your unique situation and options.

Contents

"Make the most of yourself, for that is all there is of you."

– Ralph Waldo Emerson

Get Rolling!

The simplest actions often make the greatest positive differences. Spending just a few minutes lying or sitting and playfully rolling on a cylinder-shaped piece of foam can help your body feel more relaxed, aligned, and resilient. The PRO-ROLLER has an ideal shape and surface for massage and soft-tissue release, encouraging tight areas to soften and lengthen. Rolling inspires increased awareness of how your body feels and moves, cultivating better posture and body symmetry while reinforcing core strength and balance.

Cylindrical-shaped foam rollers that once served only as packing material have now been adapted and adopted by physical therapists, movement educators, and fitness instructors throughout the world. Dr. Moshe Feldenkrais (1902–1984), physicist and founder of the Feldenkrais Method, was one of the first people to begin using foam rollers as a therapeutic device. Rehabilitation professionals utilize foam rollers for muscle reeducation, dynamic strengthening, enhancing balance reactions, increasing flexibility of muscles and nerves, and challenging sensory and movement systems.

Foam roller manufacturing has improved over time to offer high-quality, long-lasting rollers that maintain their shape even with heavy use. With closed-cell, heat-molded construction and durable EVA foam, the PRO-ROLLER series is both comfortable and well suited for myofascial release, balance, and stability exercises. The green and blue marble 6-inch diameter rollers feature standard density (medium firm) and are excellent for self-massage and soft-tissue release techniques.

Both blue and pink marble PRO-ROLLER Soft rollers are softer in density, providing more gentle and comfortable support for successful self-myofascial release. Research supports the use of soft foam rollers to facilitate optimized biomechanical loading of targeted tissues for effective results. And the blue marble soft roller comes in a compact 18-inch length for convenient on-the-go portability.

Using a PRO-ROLLER for self-massage helps you to target specific areas of tightness or tenderness. You are in control of the amount of pressure and time focused on each region to decrease stress and tension in muscles, fascia, and connective tissues. The rolling movements naturally encourage integration of body and mind. In response to appropriate sensory stimulus, the brain signals the muscles to relax and lengthen. With consistent use of PRO-ROLLER self-massage techniques, you will help to improve as well as prevent problems of muscle tension and soft-tissue restriction. Get ready to roll!

The PRO-ROLLER is also available with a 4-inch diameter. Purple rollers have medium-firm density, while blue marble rollers are softer. This smaller diameter makes the body lower to the floor, encourages confident use and ease of control during rolling movements, and promotes directed release of specific areas of tightness or tension.

Observation is an essential component of any self-care program. With a beginner's mind, notice how your body feels and moves before, during, and after PRO-ROLLER massaging and releasing movements. Since our brains are innately wired for alertness to negativity, your attention may be summoned to any areas of tightness or soreness. This awareness can be expanded by moving slowly and gently, encouraging self-discovery, sensing resistance, supporting release, and letting go of tension. Pausing to notice, take in the good, and record beneficial gains within your brain's map of your body will improve your positive health outcomes. Foam rolling is experiential—explore and feel, and try rolling and experiencing differently today than you did yesterday.

The body's muscles, fascia, and connective tissues function best when they are fluid and moving freely, sliding and gliding. PRO-ROLLER self-massage techniques direct comfortable but sufficient pressure to tender areas of chronic contraction in our muscles and fascia that may feel like knots or lumps. This tightness or restriction frequently results from poor posture, inflammation, or trauma; it often feels a bit sore and sometimes causes discomfort in other body regions. Gentle, sustained pressure applied slowly allows the viscoelastic fascia to elongate, releasing superficial tightness and then deeper restrictions. As you explore rolling and experience your body's own responses, you may encounter other interrelated areas of tightness or tension.

PRO-ROLLER massage exercises are best performed on a firm, flat surface such as the floor, an exercise mat, or a low exercise table. Wear comfortable clothing so you can move freely. Leave feet bare or wear socks with a grip surface. Keep your PRO-ROLLER easily accessible, so you know you'll use it often. When not in use, store it lying flat; avoid stacking anything heavy on top that could cause dents. Use mild soap and water to clean.

As you get rolling, keep these guidelines in mind:

- Listen to your body and its own capabilities; choose only the movements that feel comfortable.
- Perform massage exercises slowly and mindfully, incorporating deep breathing to relieve muscle tension.
- Stop and rest if, during any exercise, you experience discomfort or feel light-headed or nauseous.
- Progress gradually. Start with simple movements, and build on your successes.
- Take extra care when massaging your head, neck, and spine. Do not roll over any acute injuries.

PRO-ROLLER use allows you to do self-massage exercises that feel good to your body. Always, choose movements that are fun and enjoyable!

Guiding Massage

For centuries, massage has been helping people feel good, and medical research confirms the health benefits of massage to enhance function, assist healing, and promote relaxation and wellbeing. One single massage decreases your stress hormones (Rapaport, et al., 2010). Twice-weekly moderate pressure massages improve range of motion, decrease pain, reduce depression and anxiety, and enhance immune function (Field, 2014). On a cellular level, 10-minute massages following exercise suppress inflammation, while promoting muscle recovery and healing (Crane, et al., 2012). Additional research will determine specific mechanisms and biological pathways, but the positive benefits of massage are already available.

Myofascial release is a form of massage that applies low-load, long-duration stretch to muscles, fascia, and connective tissues, helping to restore optimal length, decrease pain, and improve function. Systematic review of published randomized clinical trials confirms the emergence of myofascial release as a treatment strategy with a solid evidence base and tremendous potential (Ajimsha, Al-Mudahka, & Al-Madzhar, 2015).

Fascia, the three-dimensional continuous web of connective tissues from your head to your toes, functions together with muscles, tendons, and ligaments. Made of collagen, elastin, and water, fascia is arranged in multidirectional layers throughout the body, enveloping and supporting nerves, muscles, blood vessels, bones, and organs. This interconnected fascial network is responsive to compression and stretch, communicating movement, relaying tension, and distributing force. Fascia is dynamic and changeable, with viscoelastic properties, forming a tensional network that is inextricably linked to multiple body structures (Schleip, Findley, Chaitow, & Huijing, 2012).

Self-myofascial release using foam rollers is an active method of soft tissue mobilization that can be used at home, at the gym, or in the workplace. Researchers report significant increases in flexibility, with no decrease in muscle strength or athletic performance, after treatment with self-myofascial release techniques (Kalichman & Ben David, 2017). One study observed that just three 20-minute sessions of foam rolling—targeting quadriceps, adductors, hamstrings, iliotibial band, and gluteals—substantially enhances recovery following delayed-onset muscle soreness and also alleviates muscle tenderness (Pearcy, et al., 2015).

Warm-up routines that include dynamic movement and total-body foam rolling result in overall improvements in athletic performance (Peacock, et al., 2014). Research comparing preventive and regenerative foam rolling shows that a single session of foam rolling reduces sports-related neuromuscular exhaustion, and concludes that rolling following exercise is sufficient to prevent further fatigue (Fleckenstein, Wilke, & Banzer, 2017).

Three distinct 2015 reviews of research on self-myofascial release with foam rollers identified positive effects on range of motion and enhanced recovery, with reduced soreness/fatigue following exercise (Beardsley & Skarabot; Cheatham, Kolber, Cain, & Lee; and Schroeder & Best). These authors each note the need for additional study to define optimal timing and duration of foam rolling, and further investigation into how to best benefit those with chronic musculoskeletal pain.

A 2018 survey of allied health professionals revealed a high percentage (81%) use foam rollers in their practice (Cheatham). Physical therapists, athletic trainers, and fitness professionals prescribe roller massage for self-myofascial release to their clients for injury treatment (69%) and for pre- and post-exercise (61%). They recommend daily foam roller massage performed at the client's own pace (46%) for 30 seconds to 2 minutes per muscle group (33%). Nearly half of those surveyed prefer a full-size roller (49%), and many believe the medium-density foam rollers are most effective (48%).

Additional research outlines the advantages of soft-density foam rollers. The positive benefits of massage therapy—improved relaxation, function, strength, and reduced pain—are possible due to the body's innate ability to respond to its environment. Since the goal of massage therapy techniques is to remodel targeted tissues, this study applied engineering principles to examine mechanotransduction, the process of converting mechanical input into the body's biochemical response. While measuring the responses of fascia, connective tissues, and muscle, the best outcomes from the transfer of forces occurred with soft foam rollers rather than firmer-density rollers (Blyum, Driscoll & Eng, 2012).

Between professional massage therapy sessions, the PRO-ROLLER is a useful tool for self-massage and soft-tissue release techniques. With PRO-ROLLER massage, you have direct, convenient access to therapeutic techniques that improve the health of your entire body and allow more frequent focus on any specific area of tightness or tension. Choose a few movements to start exploring the roller techniques on different regions of your body, and gradually expand your repertoire to encourage whole-body integration.

Try combining PRO-ROLLER massage techniques along with your regular exercise workouts. Rolling prior to exercise relieves body tension and muscle imbalances and promotes exercise that effectively trains your body with balanced strength and flexibility. Roll after your workout to decrease muscle soreness and help prevent problems or injuries, and at the end of your workday to relieve stress and tension of tightened or overused muscles.

Listen to your body! Know that you are the best expert on what you are feeling and experiencing. Massage each region for a minute or two by rolling with slow, controlled movements. If you notice an area of tightness or tenderness, use smaller targeted movements or pause for a few deep breaths to encourage the tissue to relax and release. Explore a variety of angles and amounts of pressure, experiment with actively moving the body part while rolling, and then rhythmically alternate movements into a massage medley. Imagine tight muscles, fascia, and connective tissues softening and lengthening, like butter melting or taffy pulling.

Remember to move slowly and gently, and avoid any soreness or irritation that may result from overworking one spot. Do not roll directly on joints or bony regions. Utilize your core muscles to support your body during the movements and while transitioning from one exercise to another. Breathe fully and deeply throughout the movements, with focus on exhaling completely in order to encourage the release of body tension and maximize the benefits of PRO-ROLLER massage.

PRO-ROLLER Massage Essentials movements utilize the roller in a variety of positions: sitting, standing, kneeling, on hands and knees, or lying on one's back, front, or side.

To lie on your back on the PRO-ROLLER, first sit on the bottom edge of the roller with your hands on the floor on either side. Slowly lower your spine down onto the roller, using your arms to help control your movement. Make sure that your head and spine are fully supported on the roller.

When getting off the roller, gently roll to your side, easing onto the floor.

To change and improve your mind-body relationship requires an inward perception of your body—pausing and paying attention. Spending time simply lying on the roller provides an ideal opportunity for noticing and experiencing your brain-body systems. Begin by observing your breathing for a minute or two... then observe any areas of your body that feel tight or tense. Common areas of tension include the lower back, neck, shoulders, and middle back between the shoulder blades.

With some playful exploration, tune in to how your body feels on the PRO-ROLLER. Balancing on the dynamic rolling surface awakens your body's senses to experience heightened awareness of the position of your bones, joints, and muscles. And while exploring movement, you will start to communicate directly with your body, fully experiencing each movement and noticing how motion, even just lifting your arm, creates subtle changes throughout your entire body.

Sweep one arm out along the floor—to the side and up, as though making a snow angel, and feel how your shoulder blade rotates and glides along the back of your ribcage. As your arm arcs sideways, observe the rotational movement of your collarbone in front of your shoulder, and feel the gliding, rolling motions of your upper arm bone at the shoulder joints. These rhythms of your bones counter-rotating occur naturally throughout your body to create balanced, efficient movement (Franklin, 2012).

Think for a moment about the shoulder muscles as your arm sweeps. Each muscle is a bundle of many fibers, with individual fibers, groups of fibers, muscles, and tendons enveloped by connective tissues called fascia. When you contract a muscle, it pulls on its surrounding connective tissue through many layers that then reach the tendon, which finally pulls on the bone. Remember that no movement happens in isolation—muscles move the fascia and connective tissues before moving the bone.

Visualizing the soft-tissue structures allows you to functionally "see" beyond the muscles into the interwoven web of fascia and connective tissue, which three-dimensionally connects and supports from the surface of your body to the deepest layers. Connective tissue absorbs forces in the body, protecting joints and other structures, returning to its original shape due to its viscoelasticity. Fascia, tendons, and ligaments in your body that have been placed under tension for a long time, as with a slouched posture, may lose their abilities to rebound, yet can recover once the pressure is removed (Franklin, 2014).

PRO-ROLLER massage invites exploration of your body's muscle and connective tissue community, enhancing its resilience and elasticity. The roller helps to act as your body's instructor, communicating with your body's senses, ensuring your focus and concentration, and fully experiencing the movement of your muscles, connective tissues, bones, and joints.

Aligning

Overall goals of massage and release techniques include healthy body alignment and efficient motion, providing the basis for comfortable, confident movement throughout your daily activities—caring for yourself and others, working, and playing. Rather than being a fixed posture based on holding a certain position, alignment is flexible and free and moves without effort. Although there is no "perfect" posture, an "ideal" posture keeps the stresses on the body evenly distributed so that joints are bearing weight comfortably and muscles are working optimally. Ideal posture is not rigid and tense, but is instead lengthened and aligned, and ready for movement. Centered, balanced alignment feels good to your body and provides the basis for freedom of movement in all directions.

Many of the massage exercise positions encourage balanced spinal alignment. An ideally aligned spine runs down the center of your body, and from the side it displays three natural curves. When lying lengthwise on the PRO-ROLLER, you will be able to feel the natural spaces of the gentle "C" curve behind your low back and neck, as well as the backward "C" curve of the upper middle back supported on the roller.

Aligned spine

balanced natural curves

The PRO-ROLLER is an effective postural training tool, offering sensory feedback that encourages symmetry between both sides of the body throughout the spine as well as at the head, shoulders, ribcage, pelvis, hips, knees, ankles, and feet. Simply lying on the roller enhances your proprioception, the sensory system that provides information to your brain about your body's position and balance, as well as the amount of tension in your muscles. Improving your proprioception leads to more efficient, healthful body movement and function.

Noticing the similarities as well as the differences between the two sides of your body will help you discover muscle imbalances that have developed from everyday movement patterns. These postural habits reflect the repetitive performance of your daily tasks. Especially in cultures where sitting is prevalent, you may observe that you sit with more of your body weight toward one sitting bone, and stand more often with body weight shifted onto your right or left leg.

Awareness of your movement habits is the first step toward positive change. Such focused attention helps you to discover your opportunities for healthy improvements. The sensory feedback provided by the roller creates an optimal interactive environment for noticing and improving imbalances. Spending time lying on the roller is one method of discovery, while another is actively rolling on the roller. Experiment by rolling an area on one side, and then compare the sensation experienced when rolling the same area on the other side of your body.

Scanning Your Body

Your body is always sending messages, and pausing to consciously listen to your body helps you to hear what it's saying. The body scan is a simple method of observing your body—tuning into sensations from the outside in, and from the inside out.

Before starting your PRO-ROLLER massage session, take a few moments to "scan" your body to notice how it feels. Paying attention is an important skill to practice, and promotes effective strategies to enhance your body-mind connection. Lie on your back on the floor or an exercise mat with your arms long and legs extended, and check in with your body. Observe the natural rhythm of your breathing. Notice how your whole body feels in its entirety, and then scan parts of your body from top to bottom, beginning at your head.

- Where is each body part resting on the floor?
- Is it level, or tilting toward one side?
- Which areas feel heavy and more in contact with the floor?
- Do you notice any areas of tightness or tension?
- Which areas feel relaxed and comfortable?
- What differences do you notice from one side of your body to the other?
- Are you touching the floor evenly on both sides? Where is there more space?
- How does your breathing influence how your body rests into the floor?

Continue your scan by checking each section of your body—neck, shoulders, arms, hands, ribcage, spine, pelvis, hips, thighs, knees, ankles, and feet.

Simply be aware how each body region is feeling at this moment.

After experiencing the PRO-ROLLER massage movements, return to this position for comparison.

Centering

Benefits

Releases whole body tension; increases body awareness; enhances mind-body connection.

Starting Position

Lie on the roller, with your head supported and spine aligned. Knees bent, feet on the floor hip-width apart or slightly wider. Arms on the floor to the sides of the roller, palms facing the ceiling.

Movement Sequence

Let your arms rest comfortably. Focus on your breathing—inhaling deeply and exhaling fully for a few moments. Allow your body to lengthen and relax into the roller.

Centering your body on the foam roller embodies the ideal position for relaxed alertness, a basic principle of mindfulness training and meditation. Spending even a few minutes each day lying centered on the roller promotes the practice of mindfulness that will enhance your presence in each moment.

Breathing is an integral part of mindfulness, allowing you to focus on each moment. If you were to take only one action toward improved health and wellbeing, awareness of breathing would likely have the greatest impact. The simple practice of focusing attention to your breathing invites deeper, slower breath patterns and encourages better health, wholeness, presence, and relaxation.

Our breathing patterns often become shallow, utilizing less than half of our lung capacity and relying on secondary chest muscles. Optimal breathing is diaphragmatic—this full, natural breath pattern effectively oxygenates the body and calms the neuromuscular system.

Notice how your body position on the roller invites expansion across your chest and the front of your shoulders. This position of openness helps counteract the repetitive, forward-focused activities common in everyday living.

- Listen to your body. Allow the roller to help you notice any imbalances, movement habits, and patterns.
- Breathe deeply and exhale fully, inviting the release of any tightness and tension with each exhale.
- Observe your natural breathing pattern—rhythmic, slow, full, deep, relaxed, and flowing.
- Feel the weight of your body supported by the roller, relaxing tension, creating open spaciousness.
- If you experience any shoulder discomfort, place pillows beneath your forearms for added support.

Spine Rocking

Benefits

Releases spinal tension; increases segmental mobility; improves balance and alignment.

Starting Position

Lie on the roller, with your head supported and spine aligned. Knees bent, feet slightly wider than hip-width apart. Relax your arms on the floor to the sides of the roller.

Movement Sequence

Slowly rock from side to side, feeling the muscles alongside your spine releasing into the roller.

- Use small rocking movements first; compare the ease of rolling toward one side and to the other.
- Pause on tender regions for a few breaths, softening the tissues alongside your spine into the roller.
- Observe your body's movement patterns, and then explore larger motions rocking from side to side.
- Allow gliding motions of the shoulder blades, ribcage, hips, pelvis, and spine segments as you rock.

Neck Massage

Benefits

Releases neck tension; improves neck mobility; increases body awareness.

Starting Position

Lie on your back on the floor, and carefully rest the base of your head comfortably on the roller. Knees bent, feet hip-width apart.

Movement Sequence

Very slowly, nod your head up and down, as if saying "yes." Then explore slowly, moving your head from side to side, and in small circles, gently massaging the upper neck and base of your head. Feel the weight of your head supported by the roller, allowing muscles to relax.

- Take extra care, or avoid these movements if you have any neck symptoms or discomfort.
- Breathe deeply and move slowly to release tightness and tension, allowing your jaw to relax.
- Pause on tender regions for a few breaths, softening and melting with each exhale.
- Imagine the roller separating out your different neck muscles and spreading connective tissue.
- Notice if you can move your neck freely without experiencing any tension elsewhere in your body.

Neck Release

Benefits

Releases neck tension; increases neck mobility; improves posture.

Starting Position

Lie on the roller, with your head supported and spine aligned. Place one hand behind your head, with elbow reaching out. Reach your other arm out to the side at shoulder level, palm up. Knees bent, feet hip-width apart.

Movement Sequence

Slowly rotate your head to the side, toward your outstretched arm. Allow muscles to relax, feeling the weight of your head supported by your hand and the roller. Maintain this position for a few slow, deep breaths and then return to center. Repeat on the other side.

- Take extra care, or avoid these movements if you have any neck symptoms or discomfort.
- Breathe deeply and move slowly, imagine connective tissues softening and melting with each exhale.
- When encountering tightness or tension, very slowly perform small, gentle nodding motions.
- If comfortable, try gently bending your neck sideways; allow hand and roller to support weight of head.

Middle Back Massage

Benefits

Releases tension between your shoulder blades; improves posture and flexibility.

Starting Position

Sit on the floor with the roller behind you, and lean back onto the roller at the lower edge of your shoulder blades. Hands behind your head for support, reach your elbows toward the ceiling.

Movement Sequence

Lift your pelvis, and slowly roll up and down your middle back from the top of the shoulder blades toward the bottom of your ribcage. Experience the support of your core muscles during movements.

Variation

Stand with feet 12-15 inches away from the wall, with roller placed behind your lower mid-back region. Slowly bend and straighten hips and knees to roll the roller up and down your middle back.

- Explore your middle back region; avoid rolling onto your neck or below the bottom of your ribcage.
- Slowly roll the areas alongside the segments of your spine, releasing tightness and tension.
- Vary the angles of motion and amount of pressure as you lean your middle back into the roller.

Middle Back Release

Benefits

Improves segmental motion of your middle back; improves posture.

Starting Position

Sit on the floor with the roller behind you, and lean back onto the roller at the lower edge of your shoulder blades. Reach wide with your elbows, holding your hands behind your head for support.

Movement Sequence

Keep your pelvis on the floor, and slowly extend back over the roller, opening your chest toward the ceiling. Relax into the movement, feeling supported by the roller, and then ease slightly forward again.

Variation

With mid-back supported on the roller, slowly arc to each side by bending your spine sideways.

- Imagine your sternum softening and upper body melting over the roller, as you rest for a moment.
- Enjoy the feeling of supported extension of your middle back, releasing tensions from daily activity.
- Inhale into extension, imagining more space for your heart and lungs, then exhale and ease forward.
- Lift your pelvis and roll up or down to another segment of your spine, then repeat the movement.

Low Back Massage

Benefits

Releases tension in low back; increases comfort and flexibility; improves posture.

Starting Position

Place the roller crosswise beneath one side of your pelvis. Knees bent, feet flat in front of you, with your forearm on the floor behind the roller to support your upper body.

Movement Sequence

Reach your other arm to your knee, slightly rotating your torso. Gently roll the roller up and down next to your spine at your lower back. Repeat on the other side.

Variation

Stand with feet 12-15 inches away from the wall, with roller placed behind lower back region. Slowly bend and straighten hips and knees to roll the roller up and down your low back.

- Take extra care, or avoid these movements if you have any low back symptoms or discomfort.
- Slowly explore the area alongside lumbar segments of your spine, releasing tightness and tension.
- Vary the angles of motion and amount of pressure as you lean your low back into the roller.

Low Back Release

Benefits

Releases lower back tension; promotes segmental spinal mobility; improves posture.

Starting Position

Stand tall and place the roller crosswise behind your low back. Hold the roller with your arms, palms facing forward.

Movement Sequence

Gently press your arms forward and arch back over the roller, adjusting roller placement for comfort. Maintain position for a few slow, deep breaths.

Variation

Kneel tall on the floor, arms hold the roller behind your low back.

- Take extra care, or avoid these movements if you have any low back symptoms or leg tingling.
- Press gently into the roller, allowing the roller to support and assist you into spinal extension.
- Extend evenly through your spine, allowing your sternum to lift and shoulder blades to relax down.
- Experience more space between each segment of your spine as you lengthen your spine to vertical.

Spine Release

Benefits

Releases spinal tension; increases segmental mobility; improves posture.

Starting Position

Lie on your side, hips and knees bent, with your head supported on the roller, spine aligned. Arms outstretched in front, at shoulder level.

Movement Sequence

Reach your top arm toward the ceiling. While reaching arm out, rotate upper body and allow front of chest to open and face the ceiling. Maintain this position for a few slow, deep breaths, and try to rotate upper body a little further. Then with core support, rotate upper body back to starting position. Repeat on the other side.

- Allow your eyes to follow the movement of your hand, rotating your spine while the pelvis counter-rotates.
- Imagine your upper body rotating in the opposite direction of your lower body, as if wringing out a towel.
- Breathing deeply sets the rhythm of your movements, experiencing core support as you exhale.
- Allow gliding motions of shoulder blades, ribcage, segments of your spine, and pelvis as you rotate.

Shoulder Blade Massage

Benefits

Releases upper body tension; increases shoulder mobility; improves posture.

Starting Position

Sit on the floor with the roller behind you. Lean your back onto the roller at the lower edge of your shoulder blades. Hold your hands behind your head for support, reaching your elbows out.

Movement Sequence

Lift your pelvis, and gently rotate your torso to one side, leaning the inside border of your shoulder blade into the roller. Slowly roll up and down the inner edge of your shoulder blade. Repeat on the other side.

- Slowly explore the muscles between your shoulder blade and spine, breathing fully and deeply.
- Vary the angles of motion and amount of pressure as your shoulder blade leans into the rolling action.
- Pause on tender regions for a few breaths, softening and melting tension with each exhale.
- With pelvis on floor, press on/off of tight areas by rotating your upper body or bending sideways.
- Massage medley: Rhythmically, alternately roll along inner border, rotate torso, and bend sideways.

Latissimus Massage

Benefits

Releases tension alongside your body; increases low back and shoulder mobility; improves breathing.

Starting Position

Lie on your side with the roller crosswise beneath your lower armpit region, with knees bent and hands behind your head. Place your top foot in front of the bottom ankle.

Movement Sequence

Slowly roll along the outer edge of your shoulder blade and toward the ribcage, relaxing into any tight or tender regions. Repeat on the other side.

Variation

Rest your top leg on the bottom leg. Slowly rotate your torso slightly forward and backward to massage different regions.

- Slowly explore the outer edge of your shoulder blade, imagining the side of your body lengthening.
- Vary the angles of motion and amount of pressure as your shoulder blade leans into the rolling action.
- Pause on tender regions for a few deep breaths, softening and melting tension with each exhale.
- Massage medley: Alternate slowly rolling along outer border, rotating torso forward and backward.

Latissimus Release

Benefits

Releases tension alongside your body; increases low back and shoulder mobility; improves breathing.

Starting Position

Sit back on your heels, knees bent at hip-width apart. Curve your spine forward, and rest your forearms on the roller.

Movement Sequence

Gently press your forearms into the roller, and roll it slowly away from your body, lengthening the sides of your body. Maintain position for a few slow, deep breaths.

Variation

For deeper release, bend your arms and press your elbows into the roller.

- Listen to your body, only performing movements that feel comfortable and enjoyable.
- Sink your tailbone toward the floor, lengthening your lower back and the sides of your body.
- As you exhale, release any tightness or tension in your lower back, shoulders, and arms.
- If experiencing knee discomfort, try a folded blanket or pillow beneath your seat.

Back-of-Shoulder Massage

Benefits

Releases tension in muscles at back of your shoulder; improves shoulder motion and comfort.

Starting Position

Lie on your side with knees bent. Hold your head with your bottom arm, and place the roller diagonally beneath your shoulder blade.

Movement Sequence

Moving your body from your hip joints, slowly roll back and forth from your shoulder blade toward your arm. Repeat on the other side.

- Gently explore the region at the back of your shoulder, slowly releasing any tightness and tension.
- Imagine massaging through posterior shoulder muscle layers, spreading out the connective tissues.
- Pause on tender regions for a few breaths, softening and melting tissues with each exhale.
- Experience core muscle support for your body during back of shoulder massage movements.
- Think of the movement being initiated by the roller, relaxing your body weight into the roller.

Shoulder Release

Benefits

Increases shoulder and spine mobility;
improves posture;
increases body awareness.

Starting Position

Kneel on the floor, sitting back toward heels, with hands on roller.

Movement Sequence

Curve your spine as you roll the roller away with one arm, and simultaneously reach the other arm across the front of your body, rotating your torso. Maintain this position for a few slow, deep breaths. Repeat on the other side.

- Listen to your body, only performing movements that feel comfortable and enjoyable.
- Breathe deeply and move slowly, imagining tissues softening and melting with each exhale.
- Think of the movement lengthening your reach, experiencing segmental motion from your spine.
- Allow gliding motions of your shoulder blades, ribcage, and pelvis together with spine movements.

Chest Massage

Benefits

Releases chest and shoulder tension; improves posture.

Starting Position

Lie on your front with the roller diagonally beneath your underarm region. Reach your arm out and place the front of your chest on the roller.

Movement Sequence

Slowly roll across the front of your shoulder and chest, from your sternum toward your collarbone and upper arm, keeping arm relaxed. Repeat on the other side.

Variation

Rotate your arm, turning palm up, to roll different portions of your chest and shoulder.

- Gently explore the pectoral region in front of the shoulder, slowly releasing tightness and tension.
- Vary the angles of motion and amount of pressure as you relax your upper body weight into the roller.
- Slowly reach your arm out in a variety of directions, observing changes with the subtle motions.
- Imagine massaging through the muscle layers of your chest, spreading the connective tissues.
- Do not roll over chest implants or mechanical devices; stop if you experience tingling sensation.

Chest Release

Benefits

Improves shoulder mobility;
releases upper body tension.

Starting Position

Lie on the roller, aligned spine. Knees bent, feet hip-width apart. Arms on the floor to the sides of the roller, palms facing the ceiling.

Movement Sequence

Slowly sweep your arms out to the sides with palms facing up. Relax into the movement, feeling supported by the roller, allowing the front of your chest to lengthen.

Variation

Bend arms to 90 degrees, and reach elbows out to the sides, trying to touch the floor with the back of your hands.

- Feel the open spaciousness across the front of your chest and shoulders, releasing upper body tension.
- Notice rotational gliding of your shoulder blades as arms reach, with body fully supported by roller.
- Breathe deeply and move slowly, softening and melting tightness and tension with each exhale.
- Try reaching arms out in a variety of directions, as if stretching after waking up in the morning.

Triceps Massage

Benefits

Releases upper arm tension; increases shoulder and arm mobility and function.

Starting Position

Lie on your side with knees bent. Keep your bottom arm long with palm facing forward, and place the roller crosswise in back of your upper arm. Rest your head on your bottom arm.

Movement Sequence

Moving your body from your hip joints, slowly roll back and forth along the back of your upper arm from your elbow to your shoulder. Repeat on the other side.

Variation

Rotate your arm, turning palm up, to roll different portions of your triceps.

- Slowly explore your upper arm from elbow to shoulder, releasing any areas of tightness and tension.
- Vary the angles of motion and amount of pressure as your upper arm leans into the rolling action.
- Pause on tender regions for a few breaths, softening and melting tissues with each exhale.
- Experience your core muscles supporting your body during the triceps massage movements.

Biceps Massage

Benefits

Releases upper arm tension; increases elbow, shoulder, and arm mobility and function.

Starting Position

Lie on your front supported on one forearm, with the roller along the other side of your body. Reach your arm out to the side at shoulder level. Place the roller beneath the front of your upper arm, with palm facing back toward your feet.

Movement Sequence

Moving your upper body from side to side, slowly roll the front of your upper arm from your elbow to the front of your shoulder. Repeat on the other side.

Variation

Rotate your arm, turning palm up, to roll different portions of your biceps.

- Slowly explore your upper arm from elbow to shoulder, releasing any areas of tightness and tension.
- Vary the angles of motion and amount of pressure as your upper arm leans into the rolling action.
- Pause on tender regions for a few breaths, softening and melting tissues with each exhale.
- Experience shoulder and core muscles supporting your body during the biceps massage movements.

Forearm Massage

Benefits

Releases tightness in forearms; improves forearm and wrist mobility.

Starting Position

Kneel on the floor with hips flexed, and place your forearms on the roller.

Movement Sequence

Moving your body from your hip joints, gently press your forearms into the roller to move it away from you and draw it back. Roll with palms in, and then rotate palms up to roll outer forearms, and down to roll inner forearms.

Variation

Stand with the roller vertically against a wall. Press your forearm into the roller, rotating your arm to roll inner and outer forearm.

- Explore movement in all directions, lean body weight into roller as tolerated to increase pressure.
- Breathe deeply and move slowly, imagining tissues softening and melting with each exhale.
- Massage medley: Rhythmically, alternate slowly rolling your forearms with palms in, rotated up, and down.

Forearm Release

Benefits

Releases tightness in wrist extensor and flexor muscle regions; improves forearm and wrist motion.

Starting Position

Kneel on the floor with hips flexed. Place the backs of your hands on the roller, with arms long and fingertips toward the floor.

Movement Sequence

Gently reach the backs of your hands into the roller, lengthening wrist extensors, and slowly lower your body back toward your heels. Maintain this position for a few slow, deep breaths.

Variation

Place palms on roller, arms long and fingertips toward floor. Reach palms into roller as you slowly lower your body toward heels, lengthening wrist flexors.

Variation

Gently rotate your forearms to angle fingertips toward each other, and then away.

- Gently reach your wrists toward the roller as your body lowers away from the roller, lengthening forearms.
- Listen to your body, only performing movements that feel comfortable; stop if you feel any tingling.
- Imagine forearm tissues softening and lengthening like taffy, releasing tightness and tension.
- Slightly rotate your forearms to change the focus, releasing tension from different forearm regions.

Gluteal Massage

Benefits

Releases hip tension;
improves posture;
increases body awareness.

Starting Position

Sit on the roller crosswise, knees bent, feet flat in front of you, and one or both arms supporting on the floor behind the roller.

Movement Sequence

Lean to one side, rolling on your buttock, and relax into any tight or tender regions. Repeat on the other side.

Variation

Sit on the roller lengthwise, rolling your buttock from sacrum to outer hip.

- Slowly explore the gluteal region, releasing and melting any areas of tightness and tension.
- Vary the angles of motion and amount of pressure as you lean your buttock into the rolling action.
- Imagine the roller separating out the different gluteal muscles and softening the connective tissues.
- Try rolling slowly with larger motions first, then target smaller areas, and return to larger motions.

Hip Rotator Massage

Benefits

Releases hip tension; increases hip mobility; improves posture.

Starting Position

Sit on the roller crosswise, knees bent, and arm supporting on the floor behind roller. Lean to one side and place that ankle on the opposite knee, rotate your hip outward as much as is comfortable and angle your knee down toward the floor.

Movement Sequence

Slowly roll from the top of your pelvis down toward the top of your thigh, relaxing and releasing deep hip rotator muscles. Repeat on the other side.

Variation

Sit on the roller lengthwise, lean to one side with ankle crossed over onto opposite knee.

- Slowly explore behind your hip, imagining the deep hip rotator muscles softening and lengthening.
- Vary the angles of motion and amount of pressure as you lean your body into the rolling action.
- Breathe deeply and move slowly, releasing tightness and tension with each exhale.
- Press gently into tender regions, slowly rock the figure-4 shape of your lower body back and forth.
- Imagine the movement being initiated by the roller, relaxing your body weight into the roller.

Sacrum Massage

Benefits
Releases tension alongside sacrum; mobilizes pelvis and lower spine.

Starting Position
Lie on your back with roller crosswise beneath your sacrum, the base of your spine. Pelvis tilted back, shoulders relaxed with hands holding ends of the roller. Legs lifted and together, hips and knees bent.

Movement Sequence
Gently rotate lower torso, allowing both knees to lower toward the roller on one side, and then the other, relaxing and releasing the area around your sacrum.

Variation
Cross one ankle over the opposite knee. Slowly rock this figure-4 shape to one side, then the other.

- Explore the weight of your pelvis sinking into the roller, releasing areas of tightness and tension.
- Sway your bent legs toward the roller at various angles, comfortably exploring the edges of your sacrum.
- Keep your shoulder blades resting into the floor, breathing fully and deeply, keep neck and jaw relaxed.
- Pause on any tender regions for a few breaths, softening and melting tension with each exhale.

Side Release

Benefits

Releases tension in hip and spine;
promotes spinal mobility;
increases body awareness.

Starting Position

Lie on your side, bottom hip and knee bent, top leg extended and supported on roller. Bottom arm long, supporting your head, top arm alongside your body.

Movement Sequence

Rest the weight of your top leg into the roller and lift your pelvic half toward the ribcage. Then press your leg into the roller and lengthen the pelvis away from the ribcage, as your leg rolls the roller away from your body. Repeat several times on each side.

Variation

Reach your top arm overhead as your leg reaches away, lengthening and releasing alongside your body.

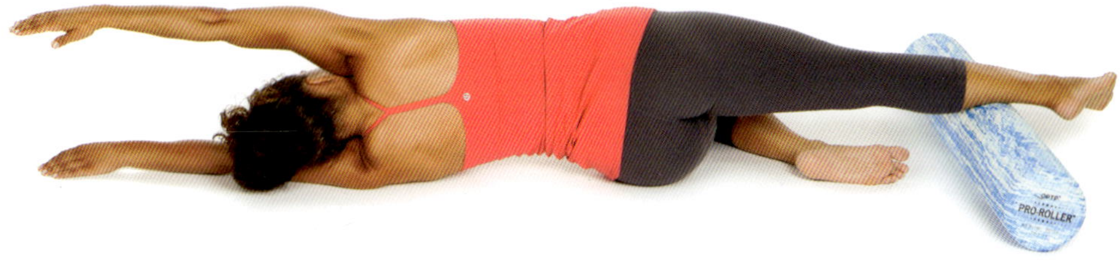

- Imagine the sides of your body lengthening, feeling spaciousness between your ribcage and pelvis.
- Experience core support as you lift the pelvic half toward the ribcage, and return to starting position.
- Breathe deeply and move slowly, releasing any tightness and tension along the sides of your body.
- Feel the gliding motions of your two pelvic halves, hip joints, and ribcage during the movements.

Outer Hip Massage

Benefits

Releases tension in outer hip;
increases awareness of pelvis and hip regions.

Starting Position

Lie on your side, with your outer hip on the roller, and your forearm supporting your upper body. Cross your top leg over the bottom leg, placing your foot on the floor.

Movement Sequence

Slowly roll down and up your outer hip region from the top of your pelvis to the top of your outer thigh. Repeat on the other side.

- Explore your outer hip region, breathing fully and deeply, releasing tightness and tension.
- Avoid excessive pressure directly onto the bony regions of your hip or pelvis as you roll.
- Vary the angles of motion and amount of pressure as your outer hip leans into the rolling action.
- Massage medley: Alternate rolling the side of your outer hip, rotating to roll slightly to front, and to back.

Variation

Rotate your body slightly toward the front as you roll, softening tight tissues.

Variation

Rotate your body slightly toward the back as you roll.

Outer Thigh Massage

Benefits

Releases tension in outer thigh, hip, and knee; improves lower body mobility.

Starting Position

Lie on your side, with your outer thigh on the roller, and your forearm supporting your upper body. Cross your top leg over the bottom leg, placing your foot on the floor.

Movement Sequence

Slowly roll down and up your outer thigh from just below your outer hip to just above your knee. Repeat on the other side.

Variation

For deeper release, place your top leg on top of the bottom leg.

- Slowly explore your outer thigh region, breathing deeply, releasing areas of tightness and tension.
- Avoid excessive pressure directly onto the bony regions of your hip or knee as you roll.
- Try slowly rolling with large motions first, then target smaller areas, and return to larger motions.
- Pause on tender regions, exploring a variety of angles and pressures to invite softening and melting.
- Massage medley: Alternate slowly rolling along your outer thigh, slightly forward, and slightly back.

Variation

Rotate out from your hip joint to roll the inner region of your outer thigh.

Variation

Turn in from your hip joint to roll the outer region of your outer thigh.

Variation

Straighten your supporting arm, changing the angle of movement and amount of pressure.

Quadriceps Massage

Benefits

Releases hip and knee tension; improves hip and knee mobility and function.

Starting Position

Place the roller beneath your thighs, with legs slightly apart, and upper body supported by elbows and forearms on the floor.

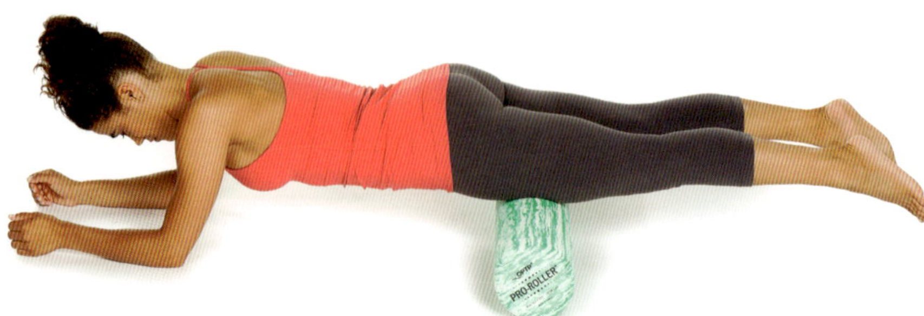

Movement Sequence

Keep your torso in one long line, and slowly roll your thighs over the roller from your hips to your knees. Move from your shoulders, pressing your forearms into the floor.

Variation

Rotate hips out to roll inner quadriceps, and then rotate in to roll outer quadriceps regions.

- Imagine the roller separating out your different thigh muscles and spreading connective tissues.
- Pause on tender regions for a few breaths, softening and melting tissues with each exhale.
- Experience core muscles supporting your body in one long line during the rolling movements.
- Massage medley: Alternate slowly rolling both thighs, bending one knee, rotating hips out and in.

Variation

For deeper release, bend one knee as you roll, and then the other knee.

Variation

With knee bent, rotate in from your hip joint to roll outer quadriceps.

Variation

With knee bent, rotate out from your hip joint to roll inner quadriceps.

Inner Thigh Massage

Benefits

Releases inner thigh and hip tension; improves hip and knee mobility and function.

Starting Position

Lie on your front supported on your forearms with the roller alongside you. Bend one hip to 90 degrees, and rest your knee and lower leg on the roller.

Movement Sequence

Slowly move your hip and pelvis from side to side, rolling up and down one-third of your inner thigh at a time. Repeat on the other side.

- Slowly explore your inner thigh region, one-third at a time: close to knee, mid-thigh, close to pelvis.
- Vary the angles of motion and amount of pressure as your inner thigh leans into the rolling action.
- Pause on tender regions for a few breaths, softening and melting any tension with each exhale.
- Focus on different regions with start position, placing your inner thigh higher or lower on the roller.
- Massage medley: Rhythmically, alternate slowly rolling part of inner thigh, bending and straightening your knee, and rotating your hip.

Variation

Add straightening and bending your knee.

Variation

Add hip rotation, turning your leg out and in from your hip joint.

Hip Flexor Massage

Benefits
Releases hip tightness and tension;
improves posture;
increases body awareness.

Starting Position
Lie on your front and lean the front of one hip on the roller, placing the opposite knee on the roller, with your forearm supporting your upper body.

Movement Sequence
Press your hip into the roller, and slowly roll the front of your hip. Repeat on the other side.

- Explore the front of your hip, rolling from near the top of your pelvis to the top of your thigh.
- Vary the angles of motion and amount of pressure as you lean the front of your hip into the rolling action.
- Imagine massaging through all the muscle layers in front of your hip, spreading connective tissues.
- Think of your hip flexor muscles relaxing, softening, widening, and melting over the roller.

Hip Flexor Release

Benefits

Releases hip tightness and tension;
improves posture;
increases body awareness.

Starting Position

Place the roller crosswise beneath your sacrum, the base of your spine. Hips and knees bent, with knees lifted.

Movement Sequence

Keep your pelvis tilting back toward the roller, and lengthen one leg out, opening across the front of your hip. Allow your foot to reach toward the floor. Maintain this position for a few slow, deep breaths. Repeat on the other side.

- Feel the open spaciousness, allowing lengthening and releasing across the front of your hip.
- Keep your pelvis tilting slightly back, feeling supported by the roller to avoid arching your low back.
- Imagine the weight of your leg as very heavy, relaxing and releasing any hip tightness and tension.
- Think of the muscles and connective tissues widening, softening, and melting with each exhale.

Sitting Bone Massage

Benefits

Releases hip and pelvic floor tension; mobilizes pelvis, hips, and lower spine; improves posture.

Starting Position

Sit on top of the roller crosswise, knees bent, feet flat in front of you.

Movement Sequence

Notice if you are sitting evenly on both sitting bones, and then shift your body weight toward one side. Slowly, gently roll alongside your sitting bone. Repeat on the other side.

Variation

Sit on the roller lengthwise, gently exploring the inner edge of your sitting bone.

- Feel the weight of your pelvis sinking into roller, comfortably exploring edges of your sitting bone.
- Vary the angles of motion and amount of pressure as you slowly roll alongside your sitting bone.
- Pause on tender regions for a few breaths, softening and melting tension with each exhale.
- Imagine creating more space and length in the soft tissue attachments at your sitting bone.

Variation

Roll near the sitting bone, flexing and then pointing your ankle.

Variation

Explore the edges of your sitting bone, rotating your leg in and out.

Variation

Sit on the roller, allowing hips to turn out, and place soles of your feet together. Shift weight to explore, gently rolling forward and back alongside your sitting bone.

Hamstrings Massage

Benefits

Releases leg tension;
improves leg and lower back
movement and comfort.

Starting Position

Place the roller beneath the back of your thighs, with your hands on the floor behind you.

➔ Movement Sequence

Slowly roll down and up the back of your thighs, from your hips to your knees.

Variation

Rotate hips out to roll outer hamstrings, and then rotate in to roll along your inner hamstrings.

- Slowly explore the back of your thighs, breathing deeply, and releasing any tightness and tension.
- Vary the angles of motion and amount of pressure as your hamstrings lean into the rolling action.
- Try rolling with large motions first, then target smaller areas, and return to larger motions.
- Massage medley: Rhythmically, alternate slowly rolling inner and outer hamstrings, back of thighs.

Variation

Roll one leg at a time, placing the other foot on the floor. Roll the back of your thigh, then rotate hip out and in.

Variation

For deeper release, roll one leg at a time by placing one leg on top of the other.

Back-of-Knee Massage

Benefits

Releases knee tension;
improves knee mobility and leg function.

Starting Position

Place the roller beneath one knee, with your hands on the floor behind you. Other knee is bent, foot flat in front of you.

Movement Sequence

Slowly roll the back of your slightly bent knee, rolling up toward your thigh and down to the top of your calf. Repeat on the other side.

- Slowly explore the back of your knee region, rolling toward your thigh, then toward the top of your calf.
- Vary the angles of motion and amount of pressure as the back of your knee relaxes into the rolling action.
- Pause on tender regions for a few breaths, softening and melting any tension with each exhale.
- Massage medley: Alternate slowly rolling the back of your knee, rotating leg out, and rotating leg in.

Variation

Roll the back of your knee over the roller with leg rotated out, and then rotated in.

Variation

For deeper release, place one leg on top of the other with ankles crossed.

Shin Massage

Benefits

Releases lower leg tension;
increases lower leg, ankle, and foot mobility;
improves posture.

Starting Position

On hands and knees, with roller placed just below your kneecaps, shoulders over your hands, hips over your knees.

Movement Sequence

Slowly bend your hips and knees to pull the roller in toward your arms and then press it back, rolling down and up your shins.

Variation

Lie on your front in plank position supported by your forearms, with roller placed under your shins. Move from your shoulders to roll shins.

- Slowly explore your shin regions, releasing and lengthening areas of tightness and tension.
- Vary the angles of motion and amount of pressure as your shins lean into the rolling action.
- Try rolling with large motions first, then target smaller areas, and return to larger motions.
- Pause on tender regions for a few breaths, softening and melting tension with each exhale.
- Experience the support of your core muscles during the shin massage movements.

Variation

Bend one leg beneath your body, extend the other leg back with shin on the roller. Slowly roll your shin over the roller, additionally exploring your hip mobility.

Variation

Slowly roll one shin over the roller with leg rotated out, and then rotated in.

Outer Calf Massage

Benefits

Releases lower leg tension; improves mobility and function of foot, ankle, and knee.

Starting Position

Lie on your side, with your outer calf on the roller, and your forearm supporting your upper body. Cross your top leg over the bottom leg, and place your foot on the floor.

Movement Sequence

Slowly roll down and up the outer calf, from just below the knee to just above the ankle. Repeat on other side.

Variation

For deeper release, place your top leg on top of bottom leg.

- Slowly explore outer calf regions, breathing deeply, and releasing areas of tightness and tension.
- Pause on tender regions, exploring a variety of angles and pressures to invite softening and melting.
- Imagine the roller initiating movement beneath your outer calf, relaxing your body weight into roller.
- Experience the support of your core muscles during the outer calf massage movements.
- Massage medley: Alternate slowly rolling outer calf, pointing and flexing ankle, rotating leg in and out.

Variation

Roll your outer calf over the roller with ankle flexed, and then pointed.

Variation

Roll your outer calf over the roller with leg rotated out, and rotated in.

Calf Massage

Benefits
Releases tension in lower legs; improves mobility and function of feet, ankles, and knees.

Starting Position
Sit on the floor, with the roller beneath your calves, and your hands on the floor behind you.

Movement Sequence
Lift your pelvis, and slowly roll up and down your calves, from your knees to your ankles.

Variation
Rotate your legs out to roll outer calves, and then rotate in to massage inner calf regions.

- Slowly explore your calf regions, breathing deeply, and releasing areas of tightness and tension.
- Pause on tender regions, exploring a variety of angles and pressures to invite softening and melting.
- Massage medley: Alternate slowly rolling your calf, pointing and flexing ankle, rotating leg in and out.

Variation

Place one foot on the floor, and roll one calf at a time. Roll your calf over the roller with ankle flexed, and then pointed.

Variation

Rotate your leg in to roll inner calf, and then out to roll outer calf.

Variation

For deeper release, roll one calf at a time by placing one leg on top of the other.

Foot Massage

Benefits

Releases tension in foot muscles; prepares feet for weight bearing and walking on uneven surfaces.

Starting Position

Stand balanced on one leg, and place the bottom of your other foot on the roller.

Movement Sequence

Press your foot into the roller, slowly rolling your foot forward and back, from toes to heel. Then slowly rock your foot sideways across transverse arch, from big to small toe. Repeat several times with each foot.

- Push downward into the roller with as much body weight as feels relaxed and comfortable.
- Imagine massaging through all the muscle layers of your foot, spreading out connective tissues.
- If balancing is difficult, hold the edge of a counter for support or try while seated in a chair.
- Massage medley: Rhythmically, alternate rolling your foot—the bottom, outer foot, and inner foot.

Variation

Rotate leg out to roll your outer foot. Press the outside of your foot into the roller, slowly rolling your foot forward and back, from small toe to your outer heel.

Variation

Rotate your leg in from your hip to roll your inner foot. Press the inside of your foot into the roller, slowly rolling your foot forward and back, from big toe to your inner heel.

Foot Release

Benefits

Releases tension in your toes, foot, and ankle; improves balance.

Starting Position

Stand balanced on one leg in front of roller, and place the toes of your other foot on the roller.

Movement Sequence

Roll the roller by slowly flexing and extending your toes and ankle. Then gently press the top of your foot into the roller, slowly rolling from toes toward front of ankle. Repeat several times with each foot.

- Elongate the top of your foot away from your shinbone, gently pressing body weight into roller.
- Feel the front of your ankle opening and lengthening, spreading the connective tissues.
- Try bending at your toe knuckles, rock foot sideways across transverse arch from big to small toe.
- If balancing is difficult, hold the edge of a counter for support or try while seated in a chair.

Comparing

Return again to scanning your body for comparison after the PRO-ROLLER massage movements.

Lie on your back on the floor or an exercise mat with your arms long and legs extended, and check in again with your body. Notice how your body feels in its entirety, and then scan parts of your body—observing your head, neck, shoulders, arms, hands, ribcage, spine, pelvis, hips, thighs, knees, ankles, and feet.

- Which areas feel more relaxed and comfortable?
- What body parts are more in contact with the floor?
- What differences do you notice in how your body feels?

Take a moment for your body and brain to fully observe and experience, and then record any changes.

Enjoy the positive sensations of comfort and relaxation in your body.

PRO-ROLLER®

MASSAGE ESSENTIALS

THIRD EDITION

At a glance, these small photos reference each *PRO-ROLLER Massage Essentials* exercise.

Gluteal Massage
page 28

Hip Rotator Massage
page 29

Sacrum Massage
page 30

Side Release
page 31

Outer Hip Massage
page 32

Outer Thigh Massage
page 34

Quadriceps Massage
page 36

Inner Thigh Massage
page 38

Hip Flexor Massage
page 40

Hip Flexor Release
page 41

Sitting Bone Massage
page 42

Hamstrings Massage
page 44

Back-of-Knee Massage
page 46

Shin Massage
page 48

Outer Calf Massage
page 50

Calf Massage
page 52

Foot Massage
page 54

Foot Release
page 56

Be mindful to —

- Listen to your body.
- Breathe deeply and move slowly.
- Pause on tender regions.
- Imagine tissues softening and melting.
- Release tension with each exhale.

Today, I will...

Feel more relaxed, aligned, and resilient by spending just a few minutes rolling on a PRO-ROLLER to release any areas of tightness and tension in my body. Add playful exploration—notice similarities and differences between the two sides of my body and observe postural habits, then spontaneously roll and massage to restore and create healthful, efficient, and joyful movement.

References

Ajimsha, M.S., Al-Mudahka, N.R., & Al-Madzhar, J. A. (2015). Effectiveness of myofascial release: Systematic review of randomized controlled trials. Journal of Bodywork & Movement Therapies, 19, 102–112.

Beardsley, C. & Skarabot, J. (2015). Effects of self-myofascial release: A systematic review. *Journal of Bodywork & Movement* Therapies, 19, 747–758.

Blyum, L., Driscoll, M., & Eng, J. (2012). Mechanical stress transfer: the fundamental physical basis of all manual therapy techniques. *Journal of Bodywork & Movement Therapies*, 16, 520–527.

Cheatham, S.W. (2018). Roller massage: A descriptive survey of allied health professionals. *Journal of Sport Rehabilitation*, Apr 13: 1–26.

Cheatham, S.W., Kolber, M.J., Cain, M., & Lee, M. (2015). The effects of self-myofascial release using a foam roll or roller massage on joint range of motion, muscle recovery, and performance: A systemic review. *The International Journal of Sports Physical Therapy*, 10, 827–838.

Crane, J.D., Ogborn, D.I., Cupido, C., Melov, S., Hubbard, A., Bourgeois, J.M., Tarnopolsky, M.A. (2012). Massage therapy attenuates inflammatory signaling after exercise-induced muscle damage. *Science of Translational Medicine*, 4, 119–132.

Field, R. (2014). Massage therapy research review. *Complementary Therapies in Clinical Practice*, 20, 224–229.

Fleckenstein, J., Wilke, J., Vogt, L. & Banzer, W. (2017). Preventive and regenerative foam rolling are equally effective in reducing fatigue-related impairments of muscle function following exercise. *Journal of Sports Science & Medicine*, 16, 474–479.

Franklin, E. (2012). *Dynamic Alignment Through Imagery*. Champaign, IL: Human Kinetics.

Franklin, E. (2014). *Fascia Release and Balance: Franklin Method® Ball and Imagery Exercises*. Minneapolis, MN: OPTP.

Kalichman, L. & Ben David, C. (2017). Effect of self-myofascial release on myofascial pain, muscle flexibility, and strength: A narrative review. *Journal of Bodywork & Movement Therapies*, 21, 446–451.

Peacock, C.A., Krein, D.D., Silver, T.A., Sanders, G.J., & Von Carlowitz, K-P.A. (2014). An acute bout of self-myofascial release in the form of foam rolling improves performance testing. *International Journal of Exercise Science*, 7, 202–211.

Pearcey, G.E.P., Bradbury-Squires, D.J., Kawamoto, J-E., Drinkwater, E.J., Behm, D.G., & Button, D.C. (2015). Foam rolling for delayed-onset muscle soreness and recovery of dynamic performance measures. *Journal of Athletic Training*, 50, 5–13.

Rapaport, M.H., Schettler, P., Bresee, C. (2010). A preliminary study of the effects of a single session of Swedish massage on hypothalamic-pituitary-adrenal and immune system function in normal individuals. *Journal of Alternative and Complementary Medicine*, 16, 1–10.

Schleip, R. & Baker, A. (Eds.) (2015). *Fascia in Sport and Movement*. Edinburgh, Scotland: Handspring Publishing.

Schleip, R., Findley, T.W., Chaitow, L, & Huijing, P.A. (2012). *Fascia: The Tensional Network of the Human Body*. London: Elsevier.

Schroeder, A.N. & Best, T.M. (2015). Is self myofascial release an effective preexercise and recovery strategy? A literature review. *Current Sports Medicine Report*, 14(3), 200–8.

Acknowledgments

The author extends tremendous gratitude to her family and friends, especially to sons, Quinn and Zane Sullivan, who continually inspire exploration, love, and laughter. Special thanks also to James E. Mullen, MD, as well as the many professional colleagues and clients whose vision, experience, and wisdom nurture continual learning, growth, connection, and sharing.